THE HISTORY OF PET CATS

by Alicia Z. Klepeis

pogo

Ideas for Parents and Teachers

Pogo Books let children practice reading informational text while introducing them to nonfiction features such as headings, labels, sidebars, maps, and diagrams, as well as a table of contents, glossary, and index.

Carefully leveled text with a strong photo match offers early fluent readers the support they need to succeed.

Before Reading

- "Walk" through the book and point out the various nonfiction features. Ask the student what purpose each feature serves.
- Look at the glossary together. Read and discuss the words.

Read the Book

- Have the child read the book independently.
- Invite him or her to list questions that arise from reading.

After Reading

- Discuss the child's questions. Talk about how he or she might find answers to those questions.
- Prompt the child to think more. Ask: Do you have a pet cat or know someone who has one? Do you think cats make good pets? Why or why not?

Pogo Books are published by Jump!
5357 Penn Avenue South
Minneapolis, MN 55419
www.jumplibrary.com

Library of Congress Cataloging-in-Publication Data

Names: Klepeis, Alicia, 1971- author.
Title: The history of pet cats / by Alicia Z. Klepeis.
Description: Minneapolis, MN: Jump!, Inc., [2024]
Series: History of pets | Includes index.
Audience: Ages 7-10
Identifiers: LCCN 2023000228 (print)
LCCN 2023000229 (ebook)
ISBN 9798885246071 (hardcover)
ISBN 9798885246088 (paperback)
ISBN 9798885246095 (ebook)
Subjects: LCSH: Cats—Juvenile literature.
Cats—History—Juvenile literature.
Classification: LCC SF445.7 .K64 2024 (print)
LCC SF445.7 (ebook)
DDC 636.8—dc23/eng/20230201
LC record available at https://lccn.loc.gov/2023000228
LC ebook record available at https://lccn.loc.gov/2023000229

Editor: Eliza Leahy
Designer: Emma Almgren-Bersie

Photo Credits: GlobalP/iStock, cover (cat); ArtCookStudio/Shutterstock, cover (toy); ANURAK PONGPATIMET/Shutterstock, 1, 18-19; Evgenyi/Shutterstock, 3; LightField Studios/Shutterstock, 4; Ashley Swanson/Shutterstock, 5; EcoPrint/Shutterstock, 6; Natallia_hap/Shutterstock, 7; J Marshall-Tribaleye Images/Alamy, 8-9 (left); QBR/Shutterstock, 8-9 (right); titoOnz/Shutterstock, 10-11; ZUMA Press, Inc./Alamy, 12-13; Darya Lavinskaya/Shutterstock, 14; Nils Jacobi/Shutterstock, 15; John Wollwerth/Alamy, 16-17tl; Viktor Sergeevich/Shutterstock, 16-17tr; Okssi68/iStock, 16-17bl; PradaBrown/Shutterstock, 16-17br; Lufimorgan/Dreamstime, 20-21; Vladyslav Starozhylov/Shutterstock, 22tl; Eric Isselee/Shutterstock, 22tr, 22ml, 22mr; Happy monkey/Shutterstock, 22bl; Axel Bueckert/Shutterstock, 22br; gabes1976/iStock, 23.

Printed in the United States of America at Corporate Graphics in North Mankato, Minnesota.

TABLE OF CONTENTS

FURRY FRIENDS

A Siamese cat jumps onto a couch. It lies next to its owner. It purrs while she pets it. The two **bond**.

Cats used to be wild. How and when did they become pets? Let's find out!

FROM MOUSE CAT TO HOUSE CAT

Cats first lived alongside people in the Middle East more than 10,000 years ago. These cats looked a lot like today's pet cats. But they were **wildcats**.

..... **wildcat**

Mice and rats were common on farms. Like today's **barn cats**, wildcats chased and ate them. Farmers liked that the cats ate the mice and rats. The cats liked having plenty to eat.

barn cat

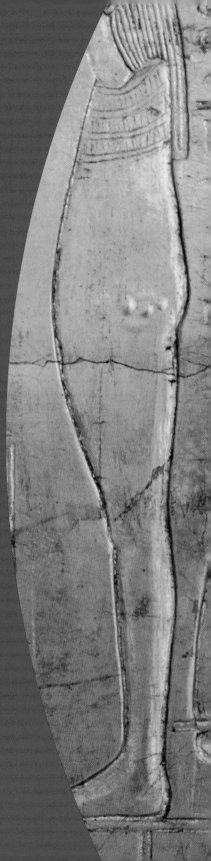

Over time, cats became less afraid of people. Some people invited cats into their homes. Cats gradually became **domesticated**.

Cats were also domesticated in Egypt. Some were even **worshipped** as gods. How do we know? They are in **ancient** carvings. People also made sculptures of them, like the cat goddess Bastet.

WHAT DO YOU THINK?

Ancient Romans saw cats as **symbols** of freedom. They let cats roam freely in their **temples** and other buildings. Why do you think cats are seen as free?

Scandinavia

Russia

Germany

Rome

Cyprus

Egypt

Sailors traveled from ancient Egypt to Rome. They brought cats on the ships. Why? Cats killed rodents on the ships. Cats spread to Europe and Russia on **Viking** ships.

WHAT DO YOU THINK?

A cat grave was found on the island of Cyprus in 2004. The grave was 9,500 years old! The cat was buried next to its owner. Cyprus does not have any **native** wildcats. How do you think the cat got there?

Starting in the 1500s, European explorers and **colonists** brought domesticated cats to the Americas. They became popular pets.

Many U.S. presidents have had pet cats. Abraham Lincoln had **tabby** cats. Rutherford B. Hayes had the first Siamese cat in the United States. President Joe Biden has a gray shorthair tabby named Willow.

Willow

CHAPTER 3

ALL KINDS OF CATS

Today, cats are the most popular pet in many countries, including Canada. They are cute and curious. They are playful and smart. They are also quiet, which is great for people in apartments.

All cats have the same wildcat **ancestors** from the Middle East. But today, there are many different **breeds**.

Some, like Himalayans, have long, fluffy fur. Others, like Bombays, have short fur. Cornish Rex cats have big ears and curly coats. Manx cats have round faces but often no tails!

Himalayan

Bombay

Cornish Rex

Manx

Many cat owners throughout history have treated their pets well. How? Some in ancient Egypt fed them fish heads. Russian kings and queens cuddled their kittens on their laps. Many cat owners do this today. We now know this is good for the cat's health. It also makes the owner happy.

TAKE A LOOK!

There are more than 93 million pet cats in the United States. In which states are people most likely to have a cat? Take a look!

① **Vermont**
② **Maine**
③ **Oklahoma**
④ **West Virginia**
⑤ **Indiana**
⑥ **New Hampshire**

Some people use toys to play with their fuzzy friends. Others give them treats. Would you enjoy having a pet cat?

DID YOU KNOW?

Cats sometimes work as **therapy** animals. How do they help? Petting them calms people. Their purring makes people feel relaxed, too.

QUICK FACTS & TOOLS

MOST POPULAR U.S. PET CAT BREEDS

1. American shorthair

2. Ragdoll

3. Maine Coon

4. Persian

5. Bengal

6. Siamese

GLOSSARY

ancestors: Early animals from which others have evolved over time.

ancient: Belonging to a period long ago.

barn cats: Cats that are semi-wild and live in barns, keeping those spaces free of rodents.

bond: To form a close relationship with someone, such as a pet or family member.

breeds: Particular types of animals that are similar in most characteristics.

colonists: People who move to and settle in a foreign place.

domesticated: Kept as a pet.

native: An animal or plant that lives or grows naturally in a certain place.

symbols: Designs or objects that stand for, suggest, or represent something else.

tabby: Cats with striped fur.

temples: Buildings used for worshipping a god or gods.

therapy: Relating to treatment of mental or physical disorders.

Viking: The Scandinavian peoples who invaded the coasts of Europe and explored the North American coast between the 700s and 1000s.

wildcats: Cats from northern Africa that scientists believe are the ancestors of pet cats today.

worshipped: Showed love and devotion to something.

INDEX

TO LEARN MORE

Finding more information is as easy as 1, 2, 3.

1. Go to www.factsurfer.com
2. Enter "thehistoryofpetcats" into the search box.
3. Choose your book to see a list of websites.

FACT SURFER